A Phoebe Chen Mystery

The Book Bandit

✳ ✳ ✳

Caron Pescatore

Illustrated by
Amanda Neves

PESKY BOOKS 4KIDZ / FORT LAUDERDALE

Copyright © 2023 by Caron Pescatore.

All rights reserved. No part of this publication may be reproduced, distributed, or transmitted in any form or by any means, including photocopying, recording, or other electronic or mechanical methods, without the prior written permission of the publisher, except in the case of brief quotations embodied in critical reviews and certain other noncommercial uses permitted by copyright law.

Cover design by Amanda Neves
https://www.amandaneves.net/

Edited by Kate Angelella
https://www.angelellaeditorial.com/

ISBN-13: 978-1958043097

Library of Congress Control Number: 2023902697

LCCN Imprint Name: Caron Pescatore, Fort Lauderdale FL

PESKY BOOKS 4KIDZ

An Imprint of Caron Pescatore, Fort Lauderdale, FL

All characters and storylines are the author's property, and your support and respect are appreciated. The characters and events portrayed in this book are fictitious. Any similarities to actual persons, living or dead, are coincidental and not intended by the author.

Printed in the United States of America

*For my husband, who has been Phoebe's biggest champion from the very beginning, insisting she needed her own series.
And for my children, the best editing team a writer could ask for!*

Table of Contents

Locker Room Looting 1

Getting Down to Business 17

The Green-Eyed Monster 29

The Lucky Duck 47

Blue's Clues 61

An Open Book 73

Read Between the Lines 85

A Squishy Situation 101

A Sour Note 123

1
Locker Room Looting

"Soccer was fun today, wasn't it?" Phoebe Chen pretended she was kicking a ball as she moved across the field.

"Yes, it was." Luana Porcello bit the inside of her cheek to keep from smiling. "And to think, *you* didn't want to join the team."

Becky Marshal's dark-brown eyes widened. "She didn't? Why not?"

Phoebe shrugged. "That's not important. I joined, didn't I?"

Luana giggled. "Phoebe hates being wrong."

"I wasn't wrong," Phoebe countered. "When you suggested we join the town team, I said I didn't think it was necessary. And it wasn't. I never said it wouldn't be fun."

"Then what did you mean when you said running around getting tired and sweaty wasn't 'your thing'?" Luana's dusky brown skin shone with sweat, and she ran a hand across her damp forehead. It was a hot, sticky day, and the sun beat down on them mercilessly.

Phoebe whirled her tiny frame around, facing her two friends. She skipped backward, her midnight-black ponytail whipping around her head as she moved.

The three girls had just finished the first of their twice-weekly soccer practice and were heading back to the locker rooms to change. The coach assigned three girls for clean-up duty each week to stay after class, help put away gear, and organize the equipment shed.

This week was Phoebe, Luana, and Becky's turn.

"I meant what I said." Phoebe stuck her nose in the air. "Getting tired and sweaty *isn't* my thing. It can, however, be quite fun." She sniffed.

Becky and Luana laughed.

"Hey, isn't that Chloe Fisher?" Luana gestured toward the parking lot behind the gigantic sports auditorium.

A skinny, brown-haired girl dashed across the lot. Chloe had her head down, and even from this distance, they could tell she was upset. They watched as she passed between two cars and disappeared from view.

"Yeah, that's her." Phoebe glanced at her wristwatch. "She's late. Practice ended forty-five minutes ago." She pursed her lips. "I wonder what she was still doing here?"

"Has it been forty-five minutes already?" Becky asked. "I have to hurry. Dad's picking me up, and he hates having to wait."

The three girls picked up speed, sprinting

toward the auditorium. The Oakdale Sports Center was a complex of four buildings in the town park. Oakdale Park was a multi-acre property on the outskirts of downtown. When they arrived at the building, Phoebe opened the door and dashed inside, making a beeline for the girls' locker room.

"Oof." She ran into something and tripped, falling forward. There was a loud crash as she felt hands grab her shoulders, pulling her back just before she hit the floor.

"Are you OK?" a female voice said.

Phoebe gasped for breath as she regained her footing. A tall, gray-haired lady steadied her. The woman's narrow face wore a severe expression belied by the twinkle in her brown eyes. Phoebe recognized her immediately. Mrs. Jonas was the weekend supervisor who oversaw the front desk activities in the sports center's administrative building next door. Phoebe steadied her breathing and smiled at the woman. "I'm sorry, Mrs. Jonas. I guess I wasn't looking where I was going."

"Tsk, tsk." Mrs. Jonas gave a slight shake of her head and smiled. "You young people are always in such a hurry."

Phoebe gave her a sheepish look.

"Hi, Mrs. Jonas," said Luana and Becky, drawing the lady's attention.

"Hello, girls." Mrs. Jonas turned to her wheeled cart with which Phoebe had collided. The basket had overturned and now lay on its side. Its contents, a mishmash of clothing, shoes, and other things, were scattered across the floor.

Mrs. Jonas righted the cart, and the girls helped her retrieve the items, replacing them in the basket. A small pink teddy bear wearing a red bowtie had slid across the floor when tossed from the cart. Phoebe hurried over to pick it up and handed it to her.

"Thank you, dear." Mrs. Jonas took the teddy bear from Phoebe's outstretched hand and placed it in the top basket of the cart. "I'm just making my usual rounds." Her eyes twinkled. "This job is becoming more dangerous by the day. Perhaps I'd better ask for hazard pay."

Phoebe cleared her throat, her cheeks growing hot. "I'm sorry, Mrs. J."

"No harm done." Mrs. Jonas wagged a finger at Phoebe. "But slow down, young lady, and look where you're going. And that goes for you two as well." She glanced at Luana and Becky.

"Yes, ma'am," said the girls.

Mrs. Jonas walked away, pushing the cart before her. The girls headed to the locker room, mindful of the woman's instruction to slow down. Once there, they retrieved their belongings to change out of their soccer gear.

They dressed hurriedly—their parents would soon arrive to pick them up.

Suddenly, a half-sobbing moan broke the silence. "I can't find it! It's gone!" Becky flung the contents of her gym bag around haphazardly, frantically searching.

"What's gone?" Luana regarded her friend with wide, amber eyes.

"My Chantal Nolan book." Chantal Nolan was a new African American children's book author. Her first novel had shot to the top of the *New York Times* bestseller list shortly after its release just over a year ago—and had remained there ever since.

"You mean that old book you've been carrying everywhere?" Phoebe tossed her head, flipping her hair over one shoulder.

"It's not an 'old book.'" Becky frowned.

Phoebe rolled her eyes. "It is so an old book—literally. You've been carrying it around all summer, and it looks beat up. I know it's your latest favorite book, but you could get another copy."

"Favorite things aren't easy to replace, Pheebs." Luana gathered her long, dark braids into a ponytail and secured it high on her head with a blue scrunchy that matched her cotton shorts. "They're like best friends. You wouldn't want me to replace *you* that easily, would you?"

Phoebe huffed. "You can't compare our friendship to a book."

Becky gave Luana a grateful look. "That's true, Luana. But this book is even more special."

"Why?" Phoebe's mouth twitched. "Can it read itself to you at night or something?"

Luana nudged her friend in the side with an elbow.

"Ouch." Phoebe rubbed her side, screwing up her face in exaggerated pain.

Luana shook her head at her friend's antics. "What makes this book so extra special, Becky?"

"Chantal Nolan autographed it!"

Luana's eyes bugged. "Really? How'd you manage that?"

"I ran into her at the airport a couple of weeks ago when we went to Georgia to visit my Grammy," said Becky. "Ms. Nolan lives in Georgia and was on the same flight. I asked her if she would sign my book, and she did.

She's ever so nice." She smiled at the memory. "She says her second book is coming out real soon. I can't wait!"

"Wow, that *is* pretty cool, Becky," said Phoebe. "When did you last see the book?

Becky shook her head. She was back to rummaging through the contents of her bag. "I was just reading it today."

"Why did you even bring it to soccer practice?" Phoebe asked.

Becky shrugged. "It was already in my bag. I had it with me when Mom took Charlie to a doctor's appointment the other day, so I read while I waited. Afterward, Mom took us to Super Slurps, and I read there too."

Phoebe scratched her jaw. She didn't get the fascination reading held for some people—except for Nancy Drew books, of course. *Those* were fantastic.

"I love Super Slurps!" Luana said. "They have the best ice cream."

"Yeah," Phoebe said. "My favorite is the chocolate caramel swirl." She smacked her lips. "Yuuummy!"

"Charlie and I love Super Slurps, too," said Becky. "Mom usually takes us there at least once a week during the summer."

"You're so lucky," said Phoebe. "I haven't been there in weeks." Her eyes lit up. "Maybe we should ask Mom to take us there now, Luana."

Luana shook her head. "There's no way Mommy Chen will let us have ice cream before lunch. And my mom is taking us to the Farmer's Market later, remember? And you always get those homemade toffees whenever we go. So, there will be no ice cream after *that* trip either."

"You're right." Phoebe sighed, then returned to their previous conversation. "So you said you last saw the book two days ago at Super Slurps?"

"No, Pheebs," said Luana. "She said she was reading it today. Try to stay focused, will you?"

"Aye, aye, Captain, ma'am." Phoebe gave a

mock salute.

Luana rolled her eyes.

"So you were reading the book today? *Here?*" Phoebe glanced around the locker room.

"Yes," Becky said. "Dad dropped me off a little early because he had an appointment. So, I read while I waited. I stuck it in my bag before going out to the field." She raised tear-bright eyes to her friends. "But it's not here now."

A slight frown creased Phoebe's forehead. "Wait a minute! You had your soccer bag with you at Super Slurps?"

"No." Becky looked confused. "Why do you think that?"

"You said you had your book with you today because it was already in your bag." Although Phoebe frequently appeared not to be paying attention, very little escaped her.

"Oh," said Becky. "It was in my messenger

bag." She picked up a small purple bag with a multi-colored peace-sign design.

"Oh, OK." Phoebe cocked her head. "And you searched that bag too?"

Becky nodded. "I did. Although, I remember sticking the book inside my soccer bag after changing into my uniform." Her voice quivered. "It's not in either bag." She looked at the mess she had created as she'd tossed her belongings around. A tear rolled down her cheek.

Luana rushed to her friend's side, wrapped an arm around her shoulder, and gave her a quick squeeze. "Don't worry, Becky. We'll help you find it. Won't we, Pheebs?" She looked at Phoebe, raising her eyebrows.

"Huh?" Phoebe's mind had returned to Super Slurps and ice cream. "Oh! Yes, yes, of course. We'll help." Her eyes widened at a sudden thought. "Ooooh, it's a mystery! We'll call it the mystery of the book bandit." She hugged herself and twirled in place.

"Book bandit?" Becky screwed up her face.

"You think someone took my book on purpose?"

Phoebe shrugged. "We won't know that until Luana and I investigate." She beamed at the thought.

Suddenly, a voice floated in from outside. "Girls, are you almost ready to leave?"

"We'll be right there," Phoebe yelled. "I forgot about Mom!" She clapped a palm to her forehead. "Luana and I have to go, Becky. How about we come by your house later, after we get back from the Farmer's Market?"

"That would be great," Becky said. "I feel much better now that you two are on the case, Phoebe. I remember how you figured out what happened to Gigi's locket a few months ago."

"Oh, yeah." Phoebe grinned. "I almost forgot about that. It's been a while. The mystery of the lost locket. It was all in a day's work for a detective."

Luana giggled. "That's the name Phoebe gave the case after she solved it," she told Becky. "Pheebs, we'd better hurry before Mommy Chen barges in here."

"My dad's probably waiting for me, too," Becky said.

Luana and Phoebe helped Becky stuff her belongings back into her soccer bag.

"Here you go." Phoebe picked up a piece of blue cloth lying on the floor under a bench and held it out to Becky.

Becky sniffled, barely glancing at the material. "That's not mine."

"Oh." Phoebe studied the cloth she held. It was a large, square piece of light blue cotton with navy-blue stripes.

"What is it, Pheebs?" said Luana.

Phoebe held up the blue material. "It's a scarf or something. Someone will come looking for it." She dropped the cloth on the bench.

The three friends quickly grabbed their belongings and headed to meet their parents.

Phoebe's mom stood outside the door while Becky's dad waited farther down the hallway, so the girls said their goodbyes as soon as they exited the changing room.

"I'll see you later," Becky said.

"Don't worry, Becky," said Luana. "We'll find your book."

Becky smiled her thanks, and Phoebe and Luana waved goodbye to their friend.

2
Getting Down to Business

"Mom, is it OK if Phoebe and I go to Becky Marshal's house?" Luana scrambled out the back door of her mother's silver SUV.

"That's fine, dear," Mrs. Porcello said. "Just be sure to be home by dinner."

Luana glanced at her wristwatch. It was almost four-thirty. "We will."

"Thanks for taking us to the Farmer's Market, āyí P," said Phoebe, addressing Mrs. Porcello as an aunt in Mandarin.

"You're welcome." Mrs. Porcello gave her a fond smile. "I'll call your mom and let her know you're at Becky's house."

Phoebe smiled back. "Thank you. And can you tell her I said, yes, I'll be home by dinner?"

Mrs. Porcello chuckled. "Will do."

Phoebe and Luana scurried down the Porcellos' long driveway, heading to Becky's house, three streets away. Several minutes later, they arrived at the colonial-style house with its lush lawn and neat floral hedge.

"Playing soccer has been good for me," Phoebe said after they'd knocked and stood waiting on the front porch for someone to answer the door. "The walk to Becky's house didn't bother me one bit."

Luana giggled. "You're eight years old, Pheebs. That walk shouldn't bother you at all."

"True. But before you forced me to play soccer, I hated exercise."

"I didn't force you!" Luana cried indignantly.

"Did, too," Phoebe shot back. "I remember it clearly. You said, 'Pheebs, we're going to play soccer.'"

"And you said OK," Luana reminded her.

"Only because I didn't have a choice."

"How do you figure that?"

Phoebe shrugged. "Because of the two of us, you're the sensible one. So if you say we're doing something, I know it makes sense to do it."

Luana rolled her eyes. "And from that, you get I forced you?"

"Exactly." Phoebe nodded. "Because I can never go against good sense."

Luana laughed, deepening the dimples in her cheeks.

The curtain on the window by the door shifted, and Becky peeked out. She smiled when she saw the two girls, then disappeared from view. A second later, the front door swung open. "You came!" Her dark eyes shone.

"We said we would," Luana reminded her.

"Yeah, I know," said Becky. "I'm just so relieved to see you. I searched my soccer *and* messenger bags again when I got home. The book is definitely not in either of them." She led the way upstairs to her bedroom as she talked. Becky's room was in its usual meticulous state, except for piles of books stacked haphazardly on every available surface. A canopied queen-sized bed sat in

the middle of the room. Hanging on either side were gauzy bed curtains covered with blue, green, and white hearts. The comforter and window drapes also had the same heart design. A giant Spelman College poster dominated one wall.

Phoebe's shoulders slumped a little as her eyes fell on the poster. It blew her mind that Becky already knew she wanted to attend the university. In the meantime, Phoebe just wanted to get through the third grade.

The three girls made themselves comfortable. Plopping on her bed, Becky picked up a heart-shaped pillow and hugged it to her chest. Luana sat in a round bucket seat at the foot of the bed while Phoebe sank to the plush green carpet, sitting cross-legged with her back against the dresser. Becky's cat, Whiskers, lounged on a pillow beside her.

Phoebe reached into her ever-present bag, a green mini backpack covered with tiny black and white magnifying glasses, and removed a small notepad and pencil.  "OK, Becky, you said you were reading the book before soccer?"

"Yes."

"Were you reading in the locker room?" Luana asked.

Becky nodded.

"Haven't you already read that book like fifteen million times?" Phoebe gave a slight roll of her eyes.

Becky shrugged. "I like it."

"Have you ever read a book you didn't like?" Phoebe tilted her head and arched an eyebrow at her friend.

"You reread Nancy Drew books all the time, Pheebs," said Luana.

"Yes, but that's research," Phoebe countered.

"Research?" said Becky.

"They help me improve how I investigate," Phoebe explained.

Luana snorted. "Sure, Pheebs. *That's* why you read Nancy Drew books."

Phoebe nodded. "Becky, are you certain you put the book in your bag before heading to the field?"

"Yes, I did." Becky nodded her head firmly. Then she paused, bit her lip, and furrowed her brow. "At least, I *think* I did."

Phoebe gritted her teeth. "So that's a, maybe?"

Becky tugged at her t-shirt collar. "Yeah, maybe. I thought I did. I'm pretty sure, but—well, you know how Coach Harris can be. She rushed into the locker room like a tornado and hurried us out the door. I was still lacing up my cleats. I barely had time to toss my bag in the locker and slam it shut before heading out the door."

Phoebe grunted. Coach Harris was a little intense. "OK, let's assume for a minute you didn't put it in the locker. I mean, there's no way for someone to get into your locker, right?"

Heat flooded Becky's face. "Er—"

Phoebe stilled, staring at Becky. "You didn't lock your locker, did you?"

Becky swallowed hard and shook her head. "My padlock stopped working a couple of weeks ago, and I keep forgetting to tell Mom I need a new one."

Phoebe sighed.

"Did you tell anyone Ms. Nolan autographed your book?" Luana asked.

"Just Katie Hanson," said Becky.

"When did you tell her?" said Phoebe.

"I saw her at Super Slurps when I was there the other day. You know how much Katie loves reading—even more than I do. She's the one who told me about Chantal Nolan's book."

"Luana, we have to get one of our parents

to take us to Super Slurps this week," said Phoebe. "I must have some chocolate caramel swirl!" She held her stomach with both hands, an expression of agony on her face.

Luana chuckled. "Focus, Phoebe. We're here to help Becky find her book, remember?"

"Yes, yes, I know." Phoebe waved her off. "So, you saw Katie at Super Slurps?" she said to Becky.

"Yes, I ran into her, and we sat together."

"And you just volunteered the information that Ms. Nolan had signed your book?" Phoebe furrowed her brow. Somehow, that didn't seem like Becky. She wasn't the type to brag. Usually, you had to drag information out of her.

Phoebe eyed her friend. Becky wore her usual orange—it was her favorite color. Phoebe could never carry off a color like that, but on Becky, it looked terrific, enhancing her stunning ebony skin to perfection. She wore her dark, kinky curls in a short afro. Not only was Becky beautiful, but she was also brilliant.

She'd been their school's Spelling Bee champ for the last two years and had led her team to victory at the second-grade science fair the previous school year. To top it off, Becky had starred in a television commercial with a major Hollywood star they had filmed several months ago.

Despite all her accomplishments, however, Becky was one of the most down-to-earth people Phoebe knew. She was also delightful and such a great friend that you couldn't be jealous of her. She didn't brag, even when there was plenty to brag about.

"No, it wasn't like that," Becky said. "Katie had her copy of Ms. Nolan's book with her. She said it was her fourth time reading it. I had my copy and told her I'd read it several times, too. She was worried Ms. Nolan would never write another book. It's been over a year since she published her first one. I told Katie about meeting Ms. Nolan at the airport and what she said about her new book coming out soon. That's when I told her about the autograph."

"Did you tell anyone else about the autograph?" Phoebe asked.

Becky shook her head.

"Katie wasn't at practice today," Luana noted. "But Phoebe and I saw her getting into her mom's car when we arrived at the auditorium."

"Oh yeah, you guys were a little late," said Becky. "Right after we got to the field, Katie complained of a stomachache. She asked her mom to take her home."

As Phoebe listened to Becky, her pencil flew across the notebook page. "So she left *after* everyone was already on the field?"

"Yes," said Becky.

Phoebe's eyes narrowed, and she tapped the pencil against her chin. *Did Katie really have a stomachache? Or did she only pretend to have one to have an excuse to return to the locker room alone and take Becky's book?*

A smile played on Phoebe's lips. They had

their first suspect.

3

The Green-Eyed Monster

The following morning, Luana and Phoebe headed out to see Katie. She lived on the same street as Becky, a few houses down. Katie's house was a curious mix of old and new, sitting at the end of a long driveway. Tall hedges surrounding the property and several large trees in the front yard hid the big house from view on the street.

They climbed sleek stone steps to the porch, and Phoebe knocked.

The door creaked open, and a tall blond boy, about twelve years old, stood in the doorway. "Hello."

"Hi," Luana said. "We're friends of Katie's.

Is she at home?"

"Sure." The boy stepped back and held the door open. "I'm Katie's brother, Tommy. Come on in."

"Thank you," said Phoebe. "I'm Phoebe Chen. This is Luana Porcello." She gestured toward her friend.

"It's nice to meet you, Phoebe and Luana. Katie is back in her sanctuary." Tommy closed the door, then led the way down a long, gloomy hallway to a small, brightly lit room. "Hey, Katie. You've got visitors." He motioned for Luana and Phoebe to enter and gave them a friendly smile before leaving.

Katie, who had jumped when she'd heard her brother's voice, was hurriedly stuffing a book under the oversized pillow on which she was lying. "Oh, hi, girls." She bolted to her feet, and her pale face flushed a bright red. "This is a surprise."

"Hi, Katie," they said.

Phoebe eyed her intently. *What is Katie hiding?*

"Can we come in?" Luana asked from the open doorway where she stood with Phoebe.

"Of course." Katie made a sweeping gesture with her hands, indicating several large pillows of varying shapes, colors, and sizes scattered around the room. "Take a seat."

Phoebe studied the room as she plopped onto a nearby pillow. Faded wallpaper covered one wall where a desk with a computer and printer stood.

Tall book-stuffed shelves made of dark, heavy wood, with gargoyles topping each at intervals, stood against two walls,  and brand new floor-to-ceiling sliding glass doors dominated another. Phoebe thought the bookshelves were creepy-looking.

Katie sank back onto the pillow she had been lying on before their arrival. It shifted as she landed on it, causing the edge of the book she'd stuffed beneath to peek out.

Luana sat on a pillow next to Phoebe. "This is a cool room." Her eyes shone as she surveyed the area.

"Thanks." Katie grinned. "It's my private reading space."

"*Yours?*" Luana's eyes rounded.

"Well, not *mine*," Katie said. "But my brothers couldn't care less about reading, so basically, it's mine."

"That's awesome," said Luana.

"Katie, we have a few questions for you," Phoebe said, getting to the point.

Luana sighed.

Phoebe held back an eye roll. They weren't there for a social visit!

"OK," Katie said. "What about?"

"It's about Becky's book," Luana said. "The one by Chantal Nolan."

"What about it?"

"Chantal Nolan autographed the book." Phoebe studied Katie through narrowed eyes as she spoke.

Katie turned to stare out the sliding glass doors, a slight frown marring her features. "I know." Her voice sounded strained. "Becky told me. What about it?" She glanced back at the two girls.

"Becky can't find it," said Luana.

"You mean she lost it?" Katie's mouth slacked.

"We're not sure what happened," Phoebe said. "But we're helping her look for it and wondered if you knew anything about it."

"Why would I?" Katie curled her upper lip.

"Becky had the book at soccer yesterday," said Luana. "She was reading it before practice."

Katie shook her head. "How could Becky be so careless? I told her she needed to put the signed copy away and buy another to read. But you know Becky; she always knows best." She sneered. "Do you know what she said when I told her I keep my autographed books locked away for safekeeping?" She glowered at Phoebe and Luana. "Well, do you?"

"Ah, no?" Luana made a vague gesture with her hand. "What—what did she say?"

"She said, 'What's the point of owning a

book if you never read it?' Now, I ask you, isn't that the stupidest thing you've ever heard?" Katie snorted and sprung to her feet. She walked to a bookshelf and slid open the door to an enclosed compartment on it. "Here are my autographed books." A note of pride filled her voice.

Phoebe and Luana exchanged glances before getting up and crossing the room to stand next to Katie. In the cubicle were six books, all in brand-new condition.

"Wow, you have an autographed copy of *When Dogs Fly*?" Luana's amber eyes sparkled. "I love that book!"

Katie smirked. "I stood two hours in line waiting to meet the author. He had a signing at the bookstore in the town where my grandparents live." She ran one finger lovingly down the book's spine before closing the compartment. She turned to face the other girls and crossed her arms. "I warned Becky she needed to take better care of the book. I'm not surprised she lost it." She wrinkled her nose. "If Ms. Nolan had autographed *my* book, I'd never let it out of my sight."

Phoebe studied Katie. "Did you see Becky reading the book before soccer practice yesterday?"

Katie's cheeks turned red. Avoiding Phoebe's gaze, she walked back across the room and sank onto the cushion. "No, I didn't." She glanced at Phoebe, then quickly lowered her eyes.

Phoebe waited, but when Katie said nothing more, she asked, "Did you see the book?"

"I just told you I didn't." A muscle in Katie's jaw pulsed.

Phoebe rolled her shoulders and sighed. "No, you told me you didn't see Becky reading the book. Now I'm asking, did you see *the book*?"

Katie shook her head slightly, refusing to look up.

"You're the only person who knew about Chantal Nolan autographing Becky's book," said Phoebe. "Did you take it?"

"Pheebs," said Luana.

Katie's head snapped up, her green eyes flashing. "Are you accusing me of taking Becky's book?"

"No, of course not, Katie," Luana assured her, shooting a chiding glance at Phoebe. "We're trying to help Becky find the book and thought perhaps you could help. That's all."

"So, when did you see Becky's book?" Phoebe moved to stand before Katie, ignoring Luana's disapproving look.

"What makes you think I saw it?" Katie demanded.

"You're hiding something," said Phoebe. "It's as plain as the nose on your face. You said you didn't see Becky reading the book, but you saw it, didn't you?"

Katie's face paled, then she nodded, chewing on her bottom lip. She looked at them, almost shamefaced. "Yes, I saw it. I wasn't lying when I said I didn't see Becky reading it. I didn't. When I got to practice, she was already getting dressed. Shortly after I arrived, Coach Harris made one of her sudden appearances. You know, when she comes in yelling and rushing everybody out."

Luana and Phoebe nodded.

"Yes," said Luana. "Becky told us about that."

"So, when did you see the book?" Phoebe asked again.

"It was afterward," Katie said. "I wasn't feeling well, so I left practice early."

"You just suddenly felt sick when you went to the field?" Phoebe said, raising her eyebrows.

"No," Katie snapped. "I had a stomachache before getting to practice. I thought I'd be OK but felt worse when we got outside. So I asked Mom to take me home. When I returned to the locker room to get my bag, I saw the book on the bench." Katie rubbed the tip of her nose with her left palm. "I didn't know it was

Becky's book, though."

"Was there anyone else in the locker room?" Phoebe asked.

Katie shook her head.

"And when you left, the book was on the bench?" Phoebe pinned Katie with her eyes as she asked the question.

Katie looked away from Phoebe. "Yes, it was."

There was a long silence as Phoebe considered what Katie had just told her. *Katie is hiding something,* she thought. *But what?* She stared at the edge of the book, peeking out from under the cushion where Katie had shoved it when they'd first arrived. "OK, thanks, Katie. Let's go, Luana."

Luana looked at her friend in surprise.

Katie jumped up, almost tripping over her feet in haste, and quickly led the girls back to the front door. "You were wrong, you know."

Phoebe arched an eyebrow. "About what?"

"When you said I was the only person who knew about the autograph," said Katie.

"Who else knows?" Phoebe wrinkled her forehead. "Becky said you're the only person she told."

"That might be true," said Katie. "But we were at Super Slurps when she told me about meeting Ms. Nolan."

Luana nodded. "Yes, she told us that."

"Well, while we were there, Chloe's brothers bumped into our table and knocked everything over," Katie said.

Phoebe grimaced. "Those Fisher twins are a menace."

Katie nodded. "Chloe helped us pick up our stuff. I also had my Chantal Nolan book, and both fell to the floor. Chloe picked them up. She looked inside the front cover of Becky's book." She shrugged. "I guess she was trying to see which was mine and which was Becky's. Anyway, she saw the autograph."

"How do you know that?" Luana asked.

"Because I was standing right next to her,"

said Katie. "When I saw the autograph, I told her the book belonged to Becky." She frowned. "The weird thing is, she almost seemed angry when she saw Ms. Nolan's signature."

"Angry?" Phoebe said. "Why do you say that?"

Katie shrugged again. "I don't know. It was something in her face."

"Did she say anything?" said Luana.

Katie shook her head. "She just handed the book back to me. Then she called her brothers, and they left. It was weird. They didn't even get ice cream. I could hear the twins whining about it as they were leaving. But Chloe told them to hush and ushered them out of the shop."

"That is strange," said Luana.

Katie opened the front door for them. As she and Luana stepped onto the porch, Phoebe turned back. "One last question."

Katie stiffened. "What is it?"

"What's your favorite Super Slurps ice

cream?"

Katie's eyes widened, a big grin spreading across her face. "Coconut cluster. Why?"

Phoebe grimaced. "No reason. I was just wondering."

Luana shook her head. "Phoebe's got Super Slurps stuck in her head now. Ever since Becky mentioned yesterday that she'd seen you there a few days ago."

The girls laughed, then Phoebe and Luana said their goodbyes and left.

"I can't believe Katie," said Phoebe as they headed back to Luana's house.

"You thought she was lying?" Luana frowned. "I don't know, Pheebs. Katie *could* have taken the book from the locker room, but I'd hate to think so."

"Book?" Phoebe scrunched up her nose. "I'm talking about the ice cream. How can coconut cluster be her favorite flavor? It's gross!"

Luana groaned. "Pheebs, can you please try to focus on the case?"

"OK." Phoebe sighed. "But you must admit coconut cluster is gross." When Luana rolled her eyes, she said, "OK. OK. The case. Katie sure was in a hurry to get rid of us."

"Can you blame her? You practically accused her of taking Becky's book."

"Did not," said Phoebe. "I merely told her the truth. Besides, Katie's hiding something."

"You know, Pheebs, it wouldn't hurt you to try using a little tact sometimes."

"That's your department," said Phoebe. "Daddy says a good interrogation strategy needs a good cop and a bad one. I'm the bad one. And you"—she pointed at Luana's chest—"are the good one." Robert Chen was the chief of detectives at the Oakdale Police Department. One day, Phoebe wanted to become a detective like her father.

"I see," said Luana. "Well, you make a perfect bad cop."

Phoebe gave a half bow. "Why, thank you, my friend."

Luana laughed. "You know, maybe Katie's just embarrassed because she's jealous Ms. Nolan signed Becky's book."

Phoebe pursed her lips. "Did you see her face when we told her Becky's book was missing?"

Luana nodded. "She looked disgusted."

"Yes, that's what I thought, too."

"What's our next move?" said Luana.

"We should go talk to Chloe. Katie said she knew about the autograph."

"Agreed." Luana looked at her watch. "But we can't go now. It's almost one o'clock. We promised Rosie we'd be home in time for lunch."

"OK. I can't go this afternoon, anyway. I have a dentist's appointment." Phoebe made a lemon-sucking face.

"Going to the dentist isn't that bad."

Phoebe gaped at her friend. "You are the weirdest person I know, Luana Porcello."

Luana giggled.

Phoebe allowed her mind to wander as they walked to Luana's house. She remembered they'd seen Chloe leaving the auditorium long after soccer practice had ended the day before and wondered why the girl had been at the sports center so late. Could Chloe have taken Becky's book? One corner of Phoebe's mouth lifted—a*nother suspect.*

4

The Lucky Duck

Phoebe and Luana hopped out of the back seat of Mrs. Chen's SUV and waited on the curb in front of the post office for Phoebe's mother to join them. Mrs. Chen had a few packages to mail and had promised to take the girls to Super Slurps afterward.

"I can't believe you got Mommy Chen to agree to take us to Super Slurps, Pheebs." Luana's lips curved into a wide smile. "You must have gotten good news from the dentist yesterday."

Phoebe grinned, showing off her mouthful of pearly whites. "Yep. Doctor Mimi said my teeth were perfectly healthy—no cavities. I convinced Mom I deserved a treat for doing such a good job brushing."

Luana giggled. "Well, you better keep up the good work, or your ice cream days will be over. You had four cavities last time you went to the dentist!"

Phoebe grimaced. "Don't remind me. Getting all those fillings was the worst. I hope I never have to go through anything like that again."

"Pheebs!" Luana grabbed her friend's arm. "Over there." She pointed behind Phoebe.

Phoebe spun around and saw Chloe Fisher standing on the curb in front of the dry cleaners a few yards away.

"Let's go talk to her!" She started walking toward Chloe, but Luana's tugging on her t-shirt stopped her. She turned back. "What?"

Luana inclined her head toward Mrs. Chen, who was approaching, carrying a few packages.

"Oh." Phoebe gave Luana a sheepish smile. "Mom, Luana and I are going to say hi to our friend Chloe. She's over there."

She motioned toward the girl.

Mrs. Chen was a small, slightly plump woman with rounded cheeks and the same piercing light-brown eyes as her daughter. "OK, dear. Make sure you girls stay on the sidewalk."

"We will," Phoebe and Luana promised.

Phoebe opened the post office door for her mother.

"Thank you, sweetie," Mrs. Chen said. "I'll be a little while," she added as she noticed the crowd inside.

After Mrs. Chen entered the post office, Phoebe and Luana quickly made their way to Chloe.

"Hi, Chloe," Luana said as they approached.

At the sound of her name, Chloe turned to face them. She was painfully thin, with red-brown hair and a heavily freckled face. "Hi, Luana. Hi, Phoebe." She smiled, revealing a row of crooked teeth. "What are you two doing here?" She rocked back on forth on the balls of her feet, hands in her shorts pockets.

"We're waiting for my mom. She's in the post office." Phoebe waved a hand in the post office's direction.

"I'm waiting for my mom, too," Chloe said. "She took the boys to get haircuts." She jerked a thumb over her shoulder at the barber shop behind them, next door to the dry cleaners. "Then we're going to Super Slurps."

"You were at Super Slurps just a few days ago, too, weren't you?" Phoebe asked.

Chloe nodded. "How did you know?"

Phoebe shrugged. "Katie Hanson mentioned it. We're doing an investigation."

"An investigation?" Chloe's dark-gray eyes rounded. "What kind of investigation?"

"We're helping Becky Marshal find her book," said Luana.

"Book?" Chloe wrinkled her nose. "What book?"

Phoebe's eyes fixed on Chloe. "The book she had with her at Super Slurps the other day. The one you picked up after your brothers knocked it to the floor."

"Oh, that book." Chloe looked away from Phoebe and stared across the parking lot.

"Katie said you saw Chantal Nolan's autograph in Becky's book," Luana said.

Chloe's eyes moved back to Luana. "What if I did?"

"Did you or didn't you?" Phoebe placed her hands on her hips as she continued staring at Chloe.

Chloe shifted her weight from one foot to the other. "I did." She clenched her jaw. "So what? It wasn't real."

"What do you mean, Chloe?" Luana blinked, gaping at the other girl.

Chloe snorted. "Oh, I heard Becky telling Katie Chantal Nolan had signed her book, but I didn't believe it. Not for a minute."

"So you were eavesdropping," Phoebe said.

Chloe's ears turned red. "No, I wasn't. I was standing at the counter right behind their table. I couldn't help but overhear what they were saying. They were so caught up in their dumb conversation about the book that they didn't even notice me."

"And you think Becky was *lying*?" Luana was dumbfounded.

"Of course," Chloe said. "Don't you?"

"How can you say she's lying?" said Phoebe. "You *saw* Ms. Nolan's signature. Katie told us you did."

"I saw *a* signature," Chloe corrected. "I'm sure it was fake."

"But why would Becky lie?" said Luana. "And why would she go to such lengths to convince people it was the truth?"

Chloe shrugged. "How should I know?"

"You must have some reason to believe she's lying," Phoebe said.

Chloe said nothing. She just stood there, staring back at Phoebe and Luana. Then her face hardened. "All right," she hissed. "You want to know why I think she's lying? It's because wonderful things are always happening to Becky. Haven't you ever noticed?"

Luana massaged her forehead with her left

hand. "Huh? What do you mean?"

"I mean exactly what I said," said Chloe. "Last year, she met Luke Stamos." She said it as though that explained everything.

Luke Stamos was a local teen who had risen to stardom after auditioning for a part in a new television series, *High School Adventures,* that had become very popular. The show's producers had cast Luke as the main character. Although the Stamos family had moved to Hollywood so that Luke could film the show, they still had extended family living in Oakdale, and Luke often visited his hometown.

Phoebe's jaw dropped. "That's because she did that commercial with him for the Oakdale Children's Hospital. And she didn't lie about it. The commercial is on TV."

"Well, how about when her parents took her to Bermuda when we were in first grade, and she met that senator?"

Phoebe and Luana remembered the incident well. Becky had been chasing after another hotel guest's runaway puppy. The puppy had escaped its elderly owner, who couldn't run after him. After hearing the lady's cry of distress, Becky had gone to her rescue, recapturing the runaway scamp. The elderly lady had turned out to be the invalid mother of one of their state's U.S. senators. The senator had been so impressed with Becky's actions that she had volunteered to visit their class, where *she*, not Becky, had recounted the full story of how they'd met.

Phoebe shook her head in disbelief. "Becky didn't lie about that either. The senator herself told us the story of how they met."

"Two weeks ago, she found that twenty-dollar bill on the floor when we were at soccer practice." Chloe's face wore a mutinous expression.

"And we were all right there when she found it," Phoebe snapped. Her patience, what little she had, was entirely at an end. "None of that matters. Becky can't find her book. It disappeared after soccer practice on Wednesday. Do you know anything about it?"

"Are you asking me if *I* took Becky's book?" Chloe fisted her hands at her sides.

Phoebe cocked an eyebrow. "Did you?"

"We're not accusing you of anything, Chloe," Luana said quickly, giving Phoebe a warning glance.

Phoebe wanted to get to the truth quickly but gritted her teeth and stepped back. Luana could handle the situation—at least for now.

"We spoke to Katie, and she told us Becky left her book on a bench in the locker room during practice," said Luana. "You were there on Wednesday, so we wondered if you saw it."

"Oh." Some of the tension eased from Chloe's body. "I saw Becky reading when I first arrived for practice."

"You left the sports complex long after practice ended," said Phoebe. "We saw you. What were you doing there so late?"

Chloe's face turned beet red. "I—I forgot something in the locker room and had to run back inside to get it."

"You looked upset when you were leaving," Luana said. "Didn't you find what you were looking for?"

Chloe shook her head, her eyes tearing up.

"You still haven't answered *my* question," Phoebe said. "Did you take Becky's book?"

Chloe glowered at her. "No, I didn't. It was on a bench in the locker room when I left."

"You mean after practice?" said Luana.

Chloe bobbed her head. "I guess she left it there when we went outside. Pretty careless of her, seeing that it's *supposedly* autographed."

"And you saw it on the bench?" said Phoebe.

"Yes."

"Was there anyone else in the locker room

when you left?" Luana asked.

"No," said Chloe. "Two other girls and I were the last to leave. When we left, the book was on the bench." She smirked. "It serves Becky right, losing her book. It's about time something bad happened to her."

Luana gasped. "That's a horrible thing to say, Chloe."

Chloe's face wore a pained expression. "It's the truth."

Phoebe regarded Chloe through narrowed eyes. "What about when you went back to the locker room? Was the book there then?"

"I don't know," said Chloe. "I wasn't paying attention to Becky's book. I was looking for—" She cut herself off, clenching her jaw, and glared at the two girls. "That's all I know."

"You were looking for what?" Phoebe's eyes bored into Chloe's.

"N—nothing." Chloe pressed her lips together.

Luana and Phoebe exchanged glances; Phoebe shrugged.

"Was anyone else in the locker room when you returned?" said Luana.

Chloe shook her head.

"Did you see anyone around?" Phoebe persisted.

"A boy from school," said Chloe. "Juan, I think his name is. He's in fifth grade with Becky's brother. He was lurking outside the locker room."

"Lurking?" Luana cocked her head to one side, raising an eyebrow.

Chloe shrugged. "He slammed into me right outside the girls' locker room and acted all weird."

"Weird, how?" said Phoebe.

"When he bumped into me, he dropped something—a book. I went to pick it up to give it to him, but as I bent down, he dived for it and snatched it up." She scowled. "He almost knocked me over—*again*."

"Do you know which book it was he dropped?" Luana said.

Chloe shook her head. "He snatched it up

so fast I barely saw it. He hid it behind his back and walked away backward, saying how sorry he was for almost running me over."

"Hmm, that sounds fishy," Phoebe mused. She wondered if Chloe was telling the truth. *We need to track down this Juan and hear what he says.*

"Yep. He was definitely up to no good," said Chloe. "Maybe *he* took Becky's book?"

"We don't know that he was *inside* the locker room." Luana wrinkled her brow. "And why would a *boy* be in the girls' locker room?"

"That's what we need to find out," said Phoebe.

5

Blue's Clues

"What do you think about what Chloe said?" Luana dipped a spoon into her chocolate-chip ice cream and stuck it into her mouth. Mrs. Chen had dropped them off at the ice cream shop while she made a quick trip to the grocery store in the same plaza.

Phoebe licked the ice cream dripping down the side of her sugar cone and closed her eyes. "Mmm. Yum. This caramel fudge is delicious." She smacked her lips. Instead of her favorite chocolate caramel swirl, she had tried a new flavor.

Luana chuckled. "I'm glad you like it. I was

worried when you got that one instead of your usual." Her mouth quirked. "But do you think you could focus on the case?"

Phoebe shrugged. "I'm not sure what I think about Chloe's story. That claim about this boy Juan lurking outside the locker room seems made up to me."

"Do you think so?"

"Don't you?"

Luana considered a moment. "Well, it seems farfetched that Juan could have taken Becky's book. I mean, how could he have known where to find her book in the first place?"

"Exactly," said Phoebe. "And it's like you said; why would a boy be in the girls' locker room?" She twisted her bottom lip between her fingers. "It's obvious Chloe is jealous of Becky. Did you hear the awful things she said about her?"

"I know." Luana sighed. "Poor Chloe."

"Poor Chloe?" Phoebe's mouth fell open. "I know you're always looking for the best in everyone, Luana, but not even you can defend the things Chloe said about Becky."

"Not the things she said," Luana agreed. "But it's obvious why she said them."

Phoebe scrunched her nose. "It's obvious to me. She's jealous."

Luana nodded. "I agree, but Chloe's only jealous because she's comparing her life to Becky's."

"That's usually why people are jealous of others, Lu."

Luana nibbled on her lower lip. "True. But Chloe's case is not about money, ability, or popularity. Haven't you ever noticed how lonely she seems? She's one of five siblings—three are younger than she is, and her older sister has some illness. I think Mrs. Fisher is so busy taking care of the sister that Chloe has to help by looking after the younger ones. She always has the twins with her."

"And those two are a menace to society." Phoebe screwed up her face at the thought of Chloe's twin brothers.

Luana nodded. "And Mr. Fisher is a detective like your dad—you know what long hours they usually work."

Phoebe licked her ice cream in silence for several minutes. "You're right, Lu. Now that you mention it, I have noticed Chloe rarely goes to any of our school functions or parties. And whenever I see her around, she almost always has her brothers with her." Suddenly, she reached over and pinched Luana.

"Ouch!" Luana rubbed her arm. "What'd you do that for?"

"That's for always being right and making me feel sorry for people." Phoebe stuck out her tongue at her friend.

Luana laughed. "You just hate that you're not as heartless as you'd like everyone to believe."

"Shh!" Phoebe held a finger to her lips and glanced around to see if anyone had overheard Luana's comment. "That's our secret."

Luana giggled. "My lips are sealed." Her

eyes sparkled as she pretended to turn a key, locking her mouth. Sobering, she stared at Phoebe. "Do you think someone stole Becky's book?"

"What do you think happened to it?"

Luana shrugged. "She could have lost it somewhere."

Phoebe furrowed her brow. "No matter what Katie says, it's not like Becky to be careless. Especially not with her precious books."

Luana swallowed another mouthful of ice cream and sighed. "You're right. But I'd hate to think someone purposely took it."

Phoebe shook her head. She didn't like to think someone could have taken Becky's book either and hoped their investigation would have a different outcome. But she didn't have much hope based on everything they'd learned so far. As far as Phoebe was concerned, either Katie or Chloe could have taken the book. Both were jealous of Becky, and both were hiding something.

Phoebe's mouth turned down at the corners. She knew that if either girl turned out to be the book bandit, Luana would be heartbroken. More than anything else, that bothered Phoebe.

The tinkling of the bell above the shop's door drew her attention, and she looked up to see a group of boys entering the store. They all wore the blue uniform of the cub scouts. Accompanying them were two men: one was tall with graying hair; the other was short and balding.

Phoebe recognized a tall, athletic boy as Becky's older brother. "That's Charlie Marshal," she whispered, jerking her chin in the boy's direction.

Luana looked over her shoulder and nodded. "I recognize him from school. I've seen Becky talking to him a few times. What's our next move?"

"I think we should check out the locker room," Phoebe said. "Maybe we can ask one of our parents to take us to practice early on Saturday so we can search around."

"What are we looking for?"

Phoebe shrugged.

The girls ate their ice cream and watched as the boys placed their orders.

"So your sister's been moping around the house because she lost some *book*?" The boy who had spoken sneered.

"Yeah." Charlie shook his head. "You'd think she'd lost a beloved pet or something the way she's been carrying on."

Another boy snorted. "Some people love their books." He shrugged. "I don't get it."

"Me either," a third boy piped in.

"Reading is for losers," a fourth volunteered.

"Are you calling my sister a loser?" Charlie spoke in a low, menacing tone.

The boy who had made the statement held up his hands in surrender. "Chill out, Marshal.

I didn't mean anything by it."

"Yeah, chill out, Charlie," another boy said. "Joe wasn't calling your sister a loser. Besides, Sanchez here is a book nerd, too." He jerked a thumb at a stocky, dark-haired boy and laughed.

The other boys joined in the laughter—all except Charlie.

"I am not." The Sanchez boy's face turned bright red.

"Are too," the boy retorted. "You're always sneaking around with your head stuck in a book when you think no one's looking."

Another boy nodded his head vigorously. "I've seen him."

"That's a lie," Sanchez cried. "I—I only read when I have to. Besides, I wouldn't cry over a book—even if the author had signed it."

Phoebe's ears perked up. Did the boy know about Becky's autographed book, or was his comment just a coincidence? She twisted her mouth. She didn't believe in coincidences. Her dad often told her there was no such thing when investigating a case.

"Do you know who that boy is?" she whispered to Luana.

"Which one?"

"The one they called Sanchez?" Phoebe pointed to the dark-haired boy standing next to Charlie.

"I'm not sure," Luana said. "I've seen him around at school. I think he's in fifth grade."

Phoebe made a mental note to find out who the boy was and finished her ice cream. Her mind mulled over the case as she ate while she kept one ear cocked to overhear the boys' conversation. After they'd placed their orders, the group pushed several small tables together and sat down to eat their treats. The two troop leaders sat together at another table on the other side of the shop. As Phoebe listened, she heard the boys talking about the upcoming Go-Kart Race-A-Thon. The race was an annual Oakdale event and would start in a few weeks.

"Pheebs." Luana poked her in the side.

"Mommy Chen's outside."

Phoebe looked out the window. Her mother waved to them from the curb. "Let's go." She hopped off her stool and headed toward the door with Luana.

As they passed the tables where the boys sat, Phoebe heard Charlie say, "You're coming over so we can go fishing in the morning, aren't you, Juan?"

Phoebe abruptly halted, causing Luana to bump into her.

"Pheebs!" Luana said, but Phoebe ignored her as she stared, transfixed, at the group of scouts. All the boys wore blue, navy-striped scarves around their necks. *They look just like the blue cloth I found in the locker room!*

Phoebe's eyes traveled to the boy Charlie had called Juan. Was that the boy Chloe said had almost knocked her over at the sports auditorium on Wednesday? Maybe she hadn't made up the story after all.

6

An Open Book

"Come on." Phoebe grabbed Luana by the arm, practically dragging her from the store.

"Pheebs, slow down." Luana tried tugging her arm from Phoebe's grasp.

The girls approached Mrs. Chen's SUV and scrambled into the back seat.

"Buckle up." Mrs. Chen waited until both girls had fastened their seatbelts before backing out of the parking space, maneuvering through the parking lot, and pulling smoothly into the traffic flow.

"What happened to you in Super Slurps?" Luana hissed.

Phoebe shook her head, silently signaling to Luana that they would talk about it when they were alone. Luana nodded her understanding, and the two girls chatted about general topics. Soon, they arrived at the Chens' residence and went upstairs to Phoebe's bedroom.

Phoebe had chosen several shades of purple with a touch of silver to decorate her sanctuary. A full-sized bed, nightstand, and craft table in dark oak were the only pieces of furniture in the room. A door on one wall led into a walk-in closet filled with clothes and a tall chest of drawers, while another opened into a bathroom Phoebe shared with her sister, Penny. An enormous Nancy Drew poster hung on the wall above Phoebe's bed. On another wall hung a framed Nancy Drew puzzle Phoebe had solved the previous year.

A giant half-done puzzle of a coastal town covered the craft table's surface. Lying on her nightstand was a magnifying glass.

Phoebe flung herself onto the bed and picked up her favorite teddy bear, clutching the stuffed toy close to her chest.

Luana sat, leaning her back against the headboard. "OK, Phoebe. Spill it. What happened in Super Slurps? You looked like you'd had an epiphany."

"Can't you ever talk like a normal kid?" Phoebe teased.

"You know what I mean, Phoebe Chen," Luana retorted. "You pick on me for my vocabulary, but you always know what I mean. What does that say about you, hmm?" She pursed her lips and tapped a finger to her chin.

"To answer your question, yes, I had a sudden thought. That boy—the one the others called Sanchez?"

Luana nodded. "You mean the one the other boys were teasing because he likes to read?"

Phoebe's brows drew together. "How do you know he likes to read?"

Luana shrugged. "He turned all red when the boys teased him about it. And then he tried to turn the attention away from himself by pointing out that even if he'd lost a signed book, he'd never—" A hand flew to her mouth. "Pheebs, he knows about the autograph!" A line creased her forehead. "But how?"

Phoebe gave Luana a meaningful look and nodded her head slowly. "And as we were leaving, I heard Charlie call him Juan."

Luana's mouth formed a perfect O. "Juan," she breathed. "Pheebs, do you suppose he's the boy Chloe said she bumped into at the auditorium?"

"Yes, I do. Don't you remember? Chloe said she's seen him hanging around with Becky's brother, and he's in fifth grade."

"And he knows about the autograph." Luana's eyes bugged. "Do you think he could have . . . ?" Her voice trailed off.

"Chloe said she bumped into him as she was entering the locker room to get whatever she'd forgotten. The boys' locker room is right next to the girls'. Maybe that's where Juan came from when he ran into Chloe, not the girls' locker room, as she thought."

"Yes, that's possible." Luana leaned her head against the headboard.

"But Chloe said he dropped a book and hid it from her. Why would he do that? And there's something else."

"What?"

"That blue scarf I found under the bench on Wednesday. Remember the one?"

Luana nodded.

"I think it was a Boy Scout's scarf, or whatever it's called."

Luana's mouth fell open. "What are we going to do, Pheebs?"

Phoebe rolled onto her back and stared unseeing up at her ceiling. After several moments, she spoke again. "We have to talk to Juan. I heard Charlie talking to him about going fishing tomorrow. They're supposed to meet at Becky's house at

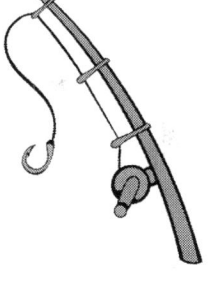

ten. We should go over there in the morning and surprise Juan before he goes inside."

"Yes, that sounds like a good plan."

The following morning, Phoebe and Luana walked to the Marshals' residence and hung around on the sidewalk, waiting for Juan. He arrived ten minutes later, riding a skateboard. Juan stopped a few feet away when he noticed them watching him. Tapping his foot on the back end of the board, he flipped it up and caught it. Then, tucking it under one arm, he approached the Marshal's gate, drawing closer to the two girls.

As he was about to turn into the driveway, Phoebe spoke. "Hello, Juan."

Juan started. "Hello? Do I know you?"

"Maybe," said Phoebe. "I'm Becky's friend, Phoebe Chen, and this is Luana Porcello."

He cocked his head and eyed the two girls.

"I think I've seen you at school." He glanced toward the house. "Are you waiting for Becky?"

"No," said Luana. "We're waiting for you."

"Me?" Juan's eyebrows shot up.

"Yes," said Phoebe. "We have a few questions for you and thought it would be better to talk out here. Alone." She shot a significant look toward the house.

Juan frowned. "What questions?"

"Did you know Becky has an autographed copy of Chantal Nolan's book?" said Luana.

Juan pressed his lips together and stared at the two girls. "Who?"

Phoebe glared at him. "Oh, please. Don't pretend you don't know who Chantal Nolan is." Hearing Luana's sigh, Phoebe bit her lip. She could almost hear Luana saying, *patience, Pheebs.* Phoebe gritted her teeth and attempted a smile. She looked more like a lion about to pounce on her prey.

Juan took a step back.

Phoebe released a heavy breath. "We know

you like to read, Juan," she said, forcing a calmness into her voice that she didn't feel. "And we know why you pretend you don't."

Juan's face paled. "What—what are you talking about?"

Phoebe made a slight sound of disgust. She'd tried, but as she'd always known, patience did not work. "Listen, here," she hissed, "you can answer our questions out here"—she pointed an index finger to a spot on the sidewalk between them—"or in there." She gestured to the Marshals' house. "It's your choice. Which will it be?"

"Pheebs." Luana nudged her gently in the side. "Juan, we don't care about your reading. Honest, we don't. I think you shouldn't have to hide something you enjoy doing. Real friends will accept you just as you are. But that's your business. Becky lost her Chantal Nolan autographed book, and we're helping her find it. Your name came up in our investigation. That's why we wanted to talk to you."

Juan leaned his head back and looked at them. "OK. I don't see how I can help, but ask your questions."

Phoebe reached into her pack and grabbed her pad and pencil. "Did you know Chantal Nolan had autographed Becky's book?"

He nodded.

"Who told you?" Luana asked.

"Charlie mentioned it when they got back from their Georgia trip," Juan said. "He said they'd met the author at the airport."

"Someone saw you at the sports center Wednesday afternoon," Luana said. "What were you doing there?"

"I had soccer."

Phoebe wrinkled her forehead. "Boys' fifth-grade soccer doesn't start until much later. I remember seeing that on the schedule. Why were you there so early?"

Juan glared at her. "My dad is the soccer coach. He has to go in early to set up for the practice."

"Oh, I see. You had a book with you." Phoebe watched as Juan's face turned beet red.

He tugged at his t-shirt collar. "I don't know who told you that, but it isn't true."

Phoebe twisted her mouth. "We're not dumb, you know. We know you had a book. The girl you almost ran over at the sports auditorium told us. She *saw* it."

Beads of sweat erupted on the boy's forehead as his eyes darted around as though he were looking for a way to escape. Phoebe moved closer, determined to stop Juan if he tried to run—although he had to be almost a foot taller than her. She could feel the excitement building inside her. Juan had to have taken Becky's book. Why else would he have hidden it from Chloe?

They were about to discover what had happened to Becky's book. Phoebe was sure of it.

Come on, Juan. Confess!

7

Read Between the Lines

Heaving a weary sigh, Juan ran a hand over his face. "OK, yes. I had a book with me, but you can't tell anyone about it. The guys would never let me live it down."

"So where is it?" said Phoebe.

"It's at my house. Why?"

"Where did you find it?" Phoebe crossed her arms and tapped a foot on the sidewalk.

"Find what?" Juan blinked.

"Becky's book, of course. What do you think we're talking about?" Phoebe said.

"What about Becky's book?" Juan furrowed his brow.

"Wasn't it Becky's book you were reading at the sports center?" said Luana.

"No, of course not," Juan said. "Why would you think that?"

"Because Becky left her book in the girls' locker room during soccer practice, and when she came back, it was gone," said Phoebe. "Somebody saw *you*"—she jabbed a finger at Juan's chest—"loitering outside the girls' locker room, and we found your neckerchief." Phoebe had looked up the correct name for the Boy Scout accessory the previous evening.

"My what?" said Juan.

"The neck thing that's part of your Scout's uniform," Luana explained.

"Oh." Juan shook his head. "It wasn't mine. My neckerchief is at home. I wore it yesterday."

Phoebe tapped a finger against her bottom lip and considered for a moment. Juan was right; he had been wearing his neckerchief when she saw him at Super Slurps the previous day. But then what—?

Juan's voice cut into her thoughts. "And I wasn't loitering. I was coming out of the boys' locker room when I ran into that girl. It was my fault. I was reading and not paying attention to where I was going. I don't know anything about Becky's book."

"But why did you hide the book from Chloe?" said Luana.

"Who?"

"The girl you ran into at the sports center."

"Oh." Juan's face reddened. "I—I—"

"Let me guess." Phoebe studied him through narrowed eyes. "You were reading some book that your *friends* would think is too girlie or babyish, right?" She made the quotes gesture as she said the word friends.

Juan licked his lips and nodded slightly.

Phoebe snorted. "Did you see anyone suspicious hanging around the building while you were there?"

"Suspicious?" Juan gave her a puzzled look.

"Yeah. You know." Phoebe shrugged. "Someone who shouldn't be there, maybe. Or someone who looked like they were up to no good."

"I think you've been reading too many mystery books." Juan's mouth twitched. "No, I didn't see any suspicious people. I only saw that girl—the one who told you about me. There were a couple of workmen and Mrs. Jonas. I'm sorry about Becky's book. I am, but I can't help you."

"Why don't you want the other boys to know you like reading?" Luana asked him.

"They know I like to read," Juan said, "and they give me a hard time about it. I don't mind it so much. It's all in good fun, but I don't do anything to draw their attention to it." He blushed. "Especially some books I like to read."

"You mean like the one you were reading on Wednesday?" Phoebe guessed.

Juan nodded. "Yes. They'd say it was a girl's

book, and I'd never live it down."

"Which book—ouch!" Phoebe cried. "What did you do that for?" She rubbed her side where Luana had nudged her.

Luana pressed her lips together and gave Phoebe a speaking glance. Making a big deal out of massaging her rib, Phoebe stuck her tongue out at her friend.

"That's just dumb, Juan," said Luana. "You should find yourself some better friends."

Juan smiled. "It's only one or two of the boys. The others couldn't care less, but—well . . ." He shrugged. "You know."

Yes, Phoebe knew. The other boys would laugh and poke fun just to keep up. She rolled her eyes. *Boys are so dumb.* "OK, well, thanks, Juan. We'll see you around."

"Bye, Juan." Luana flashed him a smile and waved goodbye as she and Phoebe took off.

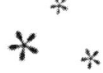

"Why'd you jab me in my side?" Phoebe demanded.

"I didn't jab you; it was a nudge. And you were about to ask Juan which book he was reading on Wednesday," said Luana.

"Yes. So?"

"It would have embarrassed him."

Phoebe rolled her eyes.

"So, what do you think?" said Luana.

Phoebe leaned back in her chair and stared at the cloudless blue sky. It was another beautiful summer day, and the girls were sitting poolside in the Porcellos' backyard. The sun shone, a blinding white-yellow ball against a deep-blue backdrop. A gentle breeze teased at Phoebe's silky black hair, lifting it gently from her face and cooling her entire body. She wrapped a lock of hair around her finger. "That caramel fudge ice cream was tasty, but I should have stuck with my usual chocolate caramel swirl." She scowled. "We're going to have to convince one of our parents to take us back to Super Slurps."

Luana rested her right elbow on the wrought-iron table and massaged her forehead with the heel of her right hand. "You're thinking about ice cream? Pheebs, can you please focus?"

Phoebe gave Luana a blank look. "What do you mean? I *am* focusing. Now, which parent can we convince to take us back to Super Slurps?"

Luana shook her head. "I meant you should focus on the *case.*"

"Oh, the case." Phoebe sighed. "All right. But we'll have to talk about ice cream later." She stared at the clear, blue-green water in the crescent-shaped pool—sunlight glinted off its surface, making the water sparkle. There was a long silence while the girls considered the case. The chirping of a family of birds who had taken up residence in the immense oak tree in the middle of the Porcellos' backyard and the constant chatter of a squirrel were the only sounds to be heard.

"OK, let's see," Phoebe said finally. "The

last time Becky saw the book was before soccer practice on Wednesday. Then, after soccer, it disappeared. That means someone had to  have taken it while Becky was on the field."

"Yes," Luana agreed. "And even if Becky had put it in her locker, it wasn't padlocked. So anyone could have taken the book."

Phoebe shook her head. "Not just anyone, Lu. I mean, why would someone try to steal a *book*?"

Luana frowned. "What do you mean?"

"I mean, it's unlikely someone would steal any old book. So, it had to be someone who knew the book's importance."

Luana's eyes widened. "Oh! You mean someone who knew about the autograph. That's what makes the book special."

"Exactly," said Phoebe. "Besides Becky's family, three other people knew about the autograph. Becky said she told only Katie about it, but Chloe knew because she was eavesdropping."

"And Juan knew because Charlie told him," Luana added.

"So, Katie, Chloe, and Juan knew," said Phoebe. "Those are our three suspects. Who is the most likely?"

"Katie seemed resentful that Ms. Nolan autographed Becky's book." Luana wrinkled her brow. "I'd hate to think Katie would do something so mean as to take Becky's book, though."

Phoebe said nothing. She didn't like the idea that one of their friends would do something so terrible either, but she'd never admit it to Luana because it would make her seem too soft-hearted. Phoebe prided herself on being the tough one.

"Katie came to soccer practice but left before it even started," she said. "Maybe she saw Becky reading the book when she arrived, then made up the stomachache as an excuse to be alone in the locker room so she could take the book."

Luana toyed with a braid and slowly nodded her head. "Yes, that could have happened." Her mouth turned down at the corners. "What about Chloe?"

"Chloe, too, could have taken it," said Phoebe. "She was still at the sports center long after she should have left. She claims she returned because she'd forgotten something but wouldn't say what. Why? What is she hiding?"

Luana slumped in her chair. "She seems so jealous of Becky."

"Yes, she is," said Phoebe. "You saw how angry she got."

Luana stared at Phoebe with troubled eyes. "Yes, she was furious."

"Then there's Juan. He was at the sports center. He could have sneaked into the girl's locker room and taken Becky's book."

"I dunno, Pheebs," said Luana. "I believed him when he said he didn't know anything about it."

"Hmm, I'm not so sure," Phoebe said. "Juan's always at the sports center early for practice because his dad's a coach. That means he had plenty of time to snoop around in the locker room."

"Do you really think so?" Luana frowned.

Phoebe shrugged. "Maybe it's something he does all the time. What do we know?"

Luana's eyes rounded. "That's a horrible thought, Pheebs."

Phoebe shrugged again. She knew Luana hated thinking badly about anyone, but Phoebe saw things like they were. Facts were facts. Sometimes kids did bad things. "So, three suspects. Which one took the book?"

Sadness clouded Luana's features. "You're convinced one of them stole it?"

"What else could have happened to it, Lu?"

Luana swallowed and gave a slight shake of her head. Her eyes were bright with unshed tears.

Phoebe sighed. "We have soccer this afternoon. Let's ask Becky if she can meet us early. We'll snoop around the locker room for clues and see if we can figure this out."

Luana and Phoebe hopped out of the back of the van. "Bye, Rosie," they chanted.

"I'll be back for you girls in an hour and a

half," said the imposing dark-skinned woman in her lilting Jamaican accent.

Rosie McDonald was the Porcellos' long-time housekeeper. "I'm just running across the street to do a few errands."

"OK," the girls said, then dashed toward the sports center.

A voice rang out behind them as they approached the building's front door. "Phoebe, Luana!"

They turned to see Becky jogging toward

them. "Hi." She waved.

"Hi, Becky." Luana stopped and waited for her friend.

"Hi, Becky." Phoebe grinned.

"Why did you want to meet early?" Becky said. "Did you find my book?"

Luana shook her head. "No, sorry."

"But we have some ideas about what could have happened to it." Phoebe pulled open the heavy glass door and stepped into the building. "Oof!" She staggered as someone slammed into her, pushing her back outside.

Luana and Becky caught Phoebe as she fell into them.

"Oh, sorry," a voice said. Then it cried, "Phoebe!" It was Chloe Fisher. She held something in her hand, which she hurriedly shoved behind her back.

Phoebe caught her breath. "Where are you off to in such a hurry, Chloe?"

"Ah, er . . . I—I forgot something in my Grandma's car." Chloe squirmed, trying to inch around the trio.

Phoebe moved, blocking her path. "You forget things a lot, don't you?"

Bright red color suffused Chloe's pale face. "I—I don't know what you mean."

"What are you hiding?" Phoebe glanced toward Chloe's arm, which she held steadfastly behind her back.

If possible, Chloe's face got even redder. "N—nothing." Deftly, she maneuvered around them and hurried toward the parking lot.

Phoebe caught sight of something pink in Chloe's hand. *What is she hiding?* She stared after Chloe with narrowed eyes when a sudden thought hit her. "OMG, guys!"

"What?" Luana stared at her wide-eyed.

"What is it, Phoebe?" said Becky.

A broad smile curved Phoebe's lips. "I think I know what happened to Becky's book."

8

A Squishy Situation

"You do?" Luana squealed.

"That's wonderful news, Phoebe," Becky said. "Where is it?"

Just then, they heard Katie Hanson's voice. "Hi, girls."

Turning, the trio saw her running toward them. "I'm so glad I'm not the only one here early!"

"Hi, Katie," they said.

"Perfect timing, Katie," Becky said. "Phoebe was just about to tell us what happened to my book."

"Oh, you found it?" Katie's eyes widened.

"Not yet," Phoebe said. "But I think I know where it is."

"Where?" Katie demanded.

"Come on." Phoebe moved away from the entrance, heading around the side of the building.

"Where are we going, Phoebe?" Becky trotted to keep up.

"You'll see." Phoebe walked down the paved walkway between the auditorium and the sports center's administrative building. Vibrant floral plants and smaller trees sat in  large planters along the path. Several tables and chairs throughout the area allowed people to sit and enjoy the nice weather. She stopped at a table and plopped her soccer bag onto a chair before turning to face the others. "Before I tell you my theory, let me explain how it came about." A big grin stretched across her face as she heard Luana groan.

"What are you girls doing out here?" Chloe's voice floated to them. Turning, the girls saw her standing at the beginning of the walkway.

"Come join us, Chloe." Phoebe waved a hand, beckoning her over.

Chloe approached, eyeing Phoebe suspiciously. "What do you want?"

"Phoebe is about to tell us where we can find Becky's book," Luana explained.

"Oh." Chloe pulled up a chair and sat at the table where the others had already taken seats. She looked at Phoebe. "Well? Where is it?"

"Patience, patience," said Phoebe. "It's thanks to you I solved the mystery."

"Me?" Chloe scrunched her face.

Phoebe nodded.

"OK, well, get to the point," Katie said.

"OK." Phoebe clasped her hands behind her back and began pacing back and forth before the girls. "It was pretty simple," she began.

Luana sighed.

Phoebe grinned. She knew Luana wanted her to get on with it, but Phoebe would do things her way. "I learned two things during this investigation. First, that new caramel fudge flavor isn't half bad. The combination of caramel and fudge go well together. But the chocolate caramel swirl is much, much better."

"What?" Becky knitted her brows. She, Katie, and Chloe stared at Phoebe as though she'd sprouted a second head.

Luana groaned. "Pheebs."

Phoebe held up her hands, palms facing forward. "All right. All right. I'll get to the case. You'd think ice cream wasn't important," she grumbled. "I'm for sure going to ask Mom to take us back to Super Slurps this week!" She released a deep breath. "OK, the case. Becky said she had her book before soccer practice. But afterward, she couldn't find it. She thought she'd left it in her locker, but obviously, she hadn't. Otherwise, the book would still be there."

"She didn't put it in her locker," Katie said. "I saw it on the bench in the locker room after Becky went out to the field. I told you that."

"Yes, you did," said Phoebe. "I was getting to that."

"Oh, sorry." Katie bit her lip.

Phoebe waved off her apology. "We figured someone had to have taken the book. But who would want to steal an old book?"

Luana coughed.

"Er, I mean, I didn't think someone would just take a book unless they knew it was special," Phoebe amended. "Like, ah, Becky's special book." Seeing Luana's approving smile, she continued. "During our investigation, we came up with three suspects. Katie, Chloe, and Juan."

"Me?" Chloe and Katie cried together.

"Juan?" Becky wrinkled her forehead. "Juan Sanchez?"

"Yes, that Juan," said Phoebe.

"But—" Becky said.

"I'll explain in a minute," said Phoebe, cutting her off. "As I was saying, Katie knew about the book and had the chance to take it. She was alone in the locker room during soccer practice. But Katie said the book was on a bench when she left. Then there was Chloe, who overheard Becky telling Katie about the autograph."

"You did?" Becky said to Chloe.

Chloe nodded. "But I didn't take it. I told you that!" She glared at Phoebe.

Phoebe ignored her. "Yes, she did," she said, answering Becky's question. "Chloe also could have taken the book because she was alone in the locker room after practice. But Chloe said she didn't take it."

"That's right," said Chloe. "I didn't."

"So Juan took the book?" Katie asked.

"I saw him with a book after practice," said Chloe. "I told Phoebe and Luana."

"What?" Becky said. "Why would Juan take my book? And how would he get it from the girls' locker room?"

Phoebe scowled. "Can I finish?"

Luana smothered a giggle.

"Chloe saw Juan with a book but couldn't say which book it was," Phoebe said. "When

Luana and I confronted him, Juan admitted he had a book but said it wasn't Becky's. He hid it from Chloe because he has this dumb hang-up about not wanting his friends to know he reads 'girlie books.'" She made the quote gesture with her fingers and rolled her eyes as she said the words.

"Poor Juan," said Becky. "Some boys give him a hard time because he's so smart."

"That just proves how dumb they are." Phoebe sneered.

The other girls nodded in agreement.

"Anyway, Juan's always early for practice because his dad's a coach. He has the run of the building. He could have gone snooping around in the girls' locker room, seen your book on the bench, and taken it," Phoebe said. "Then there's that blue cloth we found."

"What blue cloth?" Becky arched her brows.

"The one I found under the bench

Wednesday when Luana and I helped you pick up your stuff."

Luana cocked her head. "You mean the scarf?"

Phoebe nodded. "Only it wasn't a scarf."

"What was it?" said Becky.

"A neckerchief."

"A what?" Chloe said.

"A neckerchief," said Phoebe. "A Boy Scout's one, to be exact."

Becky's eyes widened. "Juan is a Boy Scout!"

"Yes," Phoebe said.

"So that was Becky's book Juan dropped when he bumped into me on Wednesday!" Chloe exclaimed.

"No, it wasn't," said Phoebe.

"Huh?" Becky scratched her nose. "But you just said—"

"Wait a minute," said Katie, cutting her off. "I'm lost. Did you say you found a Boy Scout neckerchief in the girls' locker room?"

"Yes," said Luana. "Phoebe found it. It was

under a bench."

"That must be Tommy's neckerchief!" Katie exclaimed.

"Your brother's?" The other girls stared at her.

Katie nodded. "Yeah. He's been going crazy looking for it. I must have picked it up by mistake when I packed my soccer bag. Mom washed our uniforms and put the laundry on her bed. Tommy's scout stuff got mixed in with my soccer gear. What'd you do with it?"

Phoebe held up a hand. "I'll get to that in a minute. Let me finish telling you about Becky's book first."

Katie opened her mouth to protest but quickly closed it, pressing her lips together when she saw the impatient look Phoebe gave her.

"I'll admit, when we came here today, I had no idea what had happened to Becky's book," said Phoebe. "Luana and I talked it over and decided we'd have to question all the girls who were at practice on Wednesday."

"You said I helped you solve the mystery," Chloe reminded her. "How?"

"Because of your teddy bear," said Phoebe.

Chloe shot to her feet, the blood draining from her face. "I—I don't know what you're talking about!"

"Oh, please." Phoebe scoffed. "Don't bother trying to deny it. I saw your teddy bear. It's pink with a red bow tie."

Luana furrowed her brow, biting the inside of her cheek as she thought. A sudden gleam appeared in her eyes as she jumped up. "I remember now!"

Phoebe nodded, her eyes sparkling as she held a finger to her lips, signaling Luana to say no more.

Luana shook her head but remained quiet.

"What's this about a teddy bear?" said Katie.

"Chloe forgot her teddy bear after soccer on Wednesday," said Phoebe. "That's why she came back—to look for it. Isn't that right, Chloe?"

Sinking back into her chair, Chloe wrung her hands, her shoulders slumping. "It's true," she murmured.

"What's the matter, Chloe?" Luana placed a hand on Chloe's shoulder.

Chloe's eyes shimmered with unshed tears. "You'll think I'm a baby."

"Huh?" said Becky. "Why would we think that?"

"Because I carry around Bow." Chloe's lower lip trembled, and a tear rolled down one cheek.

"Bow?" Phoebe wrinkled her forehead.

"I think that's her teddy bear's name." Luana looked at Chloe questioningly.

Chloe swallowed hard and gave a slight nod of her head.

"So what if you run around with a teddy bear?" Phoebe said. "Katie reads those ridiculous Captain Underpants books."

Now it was Katie's turn to blush. "How—

how did you know that?"

Phoebe rolled her eyes. "You tried to hide the one you were reading when we came to your house on Thursday, but I saw it under your pillow. I recognized the cover. I read that one."

"You did?" Katie's eyes bugged out. "But you just said it was ridiculous."

"It is ridiculous," said Phoebe. "That's why I like them."

The girls giggled.

"Well, I might as well confess my embarrassing secret." Becky bent over and unzipped her soccer bag lying between her feet. She rummaged inside the bag and pulled out a stuffed frog. "I bring Mr. Froggy with me pretty much everywhere. He's usually in the car, though. I guess that makes me a baby, too." She nudged Chloe gently with her shoulder.

Chloe gave her a grateful smile.

"All these dramatics over

stuffed animals are so unnecessary," Phoebe said. "My sister is fifteen and still sleeps in a bed full of stuffed toys! Of course, she hides them whenever her friends come over."

The girls burst into raucous laughter.

When she finally stopped laughing, Becky said, "But seriously, Chloe, you shouldn't feel bad about carrying Bow around. I see how hard you work, helping your mom take care of your siblings. It must be nice to have a friend to keep you company."

Chloe's eyes went round. "That is exactly what it's like, Becky! I feel so lonely, always missing out on things because I have to look after my brothers. I don't mind doing it because Dad's always working and Mom's busy with Ella, but still."

"It must be very hard," said Becky kindly. "But you know you don't have to miss out, Chloe. We can do things with you *and* your brothers."

Katie nodded, her eyes shining. "Yes! And we can help you babysit."

"You guys would do that for me?" Chloe sniffled and wiped her nose on her t-shirt sleeve.

"Of course," said Luana. "That's what friends are for, to help each other."

"Oh, thanks, you guys," said Chloe. "That means a lot to me."

Becky gave her a quick hug, then turned to Phoebe. "You still haven't explained what Chloe's teddy bear has to do with anything."

"Yes, Phoebe," said Chloe. "And how did you know I was looking for Bow?"

"I saw a flash of pink when you took off after bumping into me earlier," said Phoebe. "It reminded me of when I knocked over Mrs. Jonas' cart on Wednesday. She had a teddy bear in her basket. A *pink* teddy bear."

"I remember that," said Becky.

"That's why Chloe couldn't find him when she looked in the locker room. Mrs. Jonas had already made her rounds."

There was a long silence as the girls all considered Phoebe's words. Then Becky's eyes widened to the size of saucers. "The lost and found!"

Phoebe nodded, beaming. "That's where you'll find your book, or I'll eat my gym bag."

Becky laughed. "I'll be right back!" She jumped up and ran toward the administrative building.

"You'd better go, too, Katie," Phoebe suggested. "I'm pretty sure that's where you'll find Tommy's neckerchief. I think Mrs. Jonas missed it on her rounds that day only because it was under the bench. She's sure to have found it by now."

"Thanks." Katie sprang to her feet and dashed after Becky. A few minutes later, the two girls reappeared. Katie clutched her brother's neckerchief.

"Here it is," said Becky, waving her book triumphantly in one hand.

"Yay!" Katie high-fived Phoebe. "You did it!"

"She sure did," said Luana. "She solved *two* mysteries!"

Becky grabbed Phoebe in a hug. "Thank you, thank you, thank you."

Phoebe's face reddened. "You're welcome. I couldn't have done it without Luana."

"Yes, thank you, Luana," said Becky.

Warm color flooded Luana's cheeks. "Phoebe did all the work. All I had to do was keep her mind focused on the case and off ice cream." She tilted her head to one side. "Come to think of it, that was *a lot* of work!"

"Come on," said Phoebe. "It wasn't *that* bad." She licked her lips. "But we need to go back to Super Slurps. I must get some chocolate caramel swirl."

Luana facepalmed. "See what I mean?"

Shouts of laughter erupted.

Phoebe and Luana were back at the Chens' later that afternoon, hanging out in Phoebe's room. Luana sprawled on the floor while

Phoebe sat at her craft's desk, concentrating on the puzzle before her.

"I just had a thought, Lu," she said.

"Hmm?" Luana glanced up from the picture she was coloring.

"I think we should make this a regular thing."

"What?"

"Solving mysteries," said Phoebe.

Luana rolled over and sat up, facing Phoebe. "You mean solving mysteries like—?"

"Nancy Drew, yes!" Phoebe's eyes sparkled. "The Clue Crew Nancy Drew, of course, not the original ones. At least, not until we're older."

Luana giggled. "Well, that's good to know. I don't think I'd like chasing after real bad guys. But I was going to say, you mean solving mysteries like finding people's lost stuff the way we did for Becky?"

"Yeah, like that. I could start a file to keep my notes on each mystery, just like Dad does when working a case."

Luana nodded. "A mystery file."

"That sounds so exciting." Phoebe's eyes gleamed.

"A Phoebe Chen mystery file," Luana added, her eyes twinkling.

Phoebe gasped. "A Phoebe Chen Mystery file. I love it, Lu!"

Luana laughed. "I knew you would."

Phoebe looked at her sheepishly, then burst out laughing.

If you enjoyed this story, please ask Mom or Dad to leave a review giving it two thumbs up! Scan the QR code to go directly to the Amazon sales page.

Keep reading for a sneak peek at Phoebe's next mystery, *The Teddy Bear Terror!*

A Phoebe Chen Mystery

The Teddy Bear Terror

✶ ✶ ✶

Caron Pescatore

1

A Sour Note

"I had a great time at camp, but it's good to be home." Phoebe Chen and her best friend, Luana Porcello, walked through the trees surrounding their neighborhood park.

"Yeah. It was fun seeing Kiana, Billie, and the other girls, but I missed—"

"Shh!" Phoebe held a finger to her lips. "Do you hear that?"

"What is it?" Luana cocked her head, furrowing her brow as she listened.

Phoebe said nothing, and after a moment, Luana heard the distinct sound of someone crying. "Oh, no." She twisted a long, dark braid around her finger and bit her lip. "Someone is sad."

Phoebe changed directions, following the crying sounds, and Luana hastened after her. As the two girls reached the tree line on the playground's edge, they saw a girl sitting in the sandbox with her back to them. She was petite with ebony skin and wore her short dark hair in twists.

"That's Lindsey." Luana recognized her neighbor from across the street. "Should we go see what's wrong?"

Phoebe nodded and marched toward the girl. "Hey, Lindsey."

The little girl started and spun around to face them. "O—oh! Hi, Ph—Phoebe." She used her t-shirt to dry her tear-stained cheeks quickly.

"Hello, Lindsey." Concern filled Luana's amber-brown eyes. "We heard you crying. What's wrong?" She approached and plopped into the sandbox beside Lindsey.

"I—I." Heat flooded Lindsey's face. "It's no-nothing."

"You're crying about nothing?" Phoebe

stared at her in disbelief.

Luana gave Phoebe a chiding look. Lindsey was extremely shy; it wouldn't be an overstatement to say she was timid. Although Luana had lived across the street from the seven-year-old for over five years and had entire conversations with her, she had yet to hear Lindsey say more than a dozen words at one time. Usually, Luana talked while Lindsey smiled and listened, offering an occasional comment only when pressed. Luana placed a gentle hand on the girl's arm. "You're obviously upset about something, Lindsey. Won't you tell us what's wrong? Maybe we can help."

Lindsey bit her lip. "O—OK. I—I can't find Miss Muffin."

"Miss Muffin?" said Phoebe. "Who's that?"

"It's her teddy bear." Luana turned to Lindsey. "Where did you last see her?"

"In the park. My cousins came to visit yesterday afternoon; we were going to a movie but had a little time before we needed to leave, so we came to the park. I brought Miss Muffin with me. We weren't paying attention to the time and ended up staying too long. Aunt Lucy, my cousins' mom, came to get us, and we had to rush so we wouldn't be late for the show. I'd put Miss Muffin on that bench"—she pointed to a seat a few feet away—"while I played in the sandbox. But we left in such a hurry that I forgot all about her." Her mouth turned down at the corners. "I didn't miss her until bedtime, but I spent the night at my cousins' house and thought I'd left her at home. When I got back this morning, I turned the house upside down, looking for her, but she wasn't there. I realized I must have left her at the park and rushed over. But I've been searching for an hour, and she's not here, either—and I found this." She raised a trembling hand holding a crumpled-up Ziploc bag with a sheet of paper inside; unshed tears shimmered in her eyes.

"What is that?" Phoebe plucked the bag from Lindsey's hand before Luana could take it. Smoothing it out, she read in silence, her eyes going wide. "This is a ransom note!"

Do you want to know what happened the very first time Phoebe solved a mystery? Then check out *The Lost Locket* (A Phoebe Chen Mystery prequel.) Turn the page to find out how you can get your free copy *today*!

THE LOST LOCKET

A Phoebe Chen Mystery

Eight-year-old Phoebe Chen has her first case to crack. Can you help?

Phoebe knows she has what it takes to be an ace detective. All she needs is a mystery to solve to prove it to everyone else. So when a friend raises the alarm over a missing necklace, Phoebe jumps at the chance to crack her first case. Move over, Nancy Drew; here comes Phoebe Chen!

With the help of her BFF, Phoebe gets to work searching for clues, interviewing witnesses, and compiling a list of suspects. But when the evidence points to a friend as the guilty party, Phoebe realizes that being a junior detective isn't all fun and games. Phoebe must find concrete evidence before she points the finger.

Can she do it, or will the miscreant get away with their dastardly plot?

Scan the QR code below to subscribe to Caron Pescatore's newsletter and get your free copy of *The Lost Locket* today!

A Kids Court Whodunit

A Courtroom Mystery Series for Kids 8-12

The Doll Dilemma: Eleven-year-old Luana Porcello overhears twin siblings fighting over the destruction of a beloved doll and gets the idea to start a kids' court. Very quickly, Luana and her BFF, mystery-solving Phoebe Chen, get to work defending the accused boy against his sister's claim that he ruined her precious doll. Can they uncover the truth before the Kids' Court pronounces their client guilty?

The Go-KartAstrophe: Luana's next-door accuses his BFF of destroying his prized go-kart. Can the mystery-solving duo find out what caused the accident, or will the boys' friendship crash and burn?

The Goody Bag Goner: When new girl Rachel is accused of swiping a one-of-a-kind goody bag at a birthday party, Luana and Phoebe swap their party hats for defense ones. But Luana isn't sure she believes her client.

The Cookie Caper: A notorious sweet sneak is accused of cookie theft by his sister but insists he's innocent. Can Luana and Phoebe sift through all the suspects and find the truth?

The Music Box Mayhem: With a pile of incriminating evidence and a ticking clock, Luana and Phoebe rush to uncover the identity of the fiend show ran off with a prized family heirloom.

AUTHOR'S NOTE

Hello! Did you enjoy *The Book Bandit*? I sure hope so. Phoebe is my favorite character in my Kids' Court Whodunit series, but shh, you can't tell the others. It would cause no end of arguing. Phoebe is such a character; I just knew she should get her own series—she thought so, too. If you enjoyed this story, please ask Mom or Dad to post a review on Amazon, giving it 5 stars!

Also, if you'd like to check out Phoebe's first mystery, click on the QR code on the previous page to download a free copy of *The Lost Locket*— be sure to check with Mom or Dad first. And check out my website at https://caronpescatore.com, where I post free short stories you can read online!

I love hearing from my readers, so please connect with me on any social media platform below. I look forward to hearing from you!

Instagram: https://instagram.com/CaronPescatore
Facebook: https://facebook.com/CaronPescatore
TikTok: https://tiktok.com@CaronPescatore
Twitter: https://twitter/CaronPescatore

ABOUT THE AUTHOR

CARON PESCATORE was born in the United Kingdom. She spent her childhood in Jamaica before migrating to the United States. After practicing as a registered nurse for several years, she entered law school, getting her J.D. in 2001. She worked as an attorney for years before leaving the profession to become a stay-at-home mom—her most challenging career to date. Ms. Pescatore recently returned to law and now works for Legal Aid. Her favorite pastimes are reading, writing, and watching true-crime shows. At present, Ms. Pescatore lives in Florida with her husband and children.

Made in the USA
Columbia, SC
28 March 2023